2 taps (1/2 measure) precede music.

Haydn: Divertimento for Flute & Orchestra

Allegro moderato

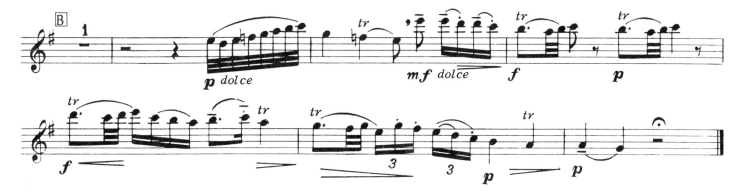

Presto

COMPACT DISC BAND AND PAGE INFORMATION

MMO CD 3304

Music Minus One

VIVALDI · HAYDN · FREDERICK "THE GREAT"
Repertoire for Flute and Orchestra

COMPLETE PERFORMANCES

		Band	Page
VIVALDI	Concerto for Flute and Orchestra *op. 10, No.3*		
	Allegro 1		1
	Larghetto cantabile 2		3
	Allegro 3		3
HAYDN	Divertimento for Flute and Orchestra		
	Allegro moderato 4		5
	Menuetto and trio 5		6
	Andante 6		6
	Presto 7		7
FREDERICK "THE GREAT"	Concerto for Flute and Orchestra		
	Allegro 8		9
	Grave 9		10
	Allegro assai 10		11

ORCHESTRAL ACCOMPANIMENT

		Band	Page
Tuning Notes A 440 11			
VIVALDI	Concerto for Flute and Orchestra *op. 10, No.3*		
	Allegro 12		1
	Larghetto cantabile 13		3
	Allegro 14		3
HAYDN	Divertimento for Flute and Orchestra		
	Allegro moderato 15		5
	Menuetto and trio 16		6
	Andante 17		6
	Presto 18		7
FREDERICK "THE GREAT"	Concerto for Flute and Orchestra		
	Allegro 19		9
	Grave 20		10
	Allegro assai 21		11

Frederick The Great: Concerto for Flute & Orchestra

12

MUSIC MINUS ONE - 50 Executive Boulevard - Elmsford, New York 10523-1325
Phone: 914-592-1188   Fax: 914-592-3116